A GIFT FOR YOU

## The Life Book, Mark Edition

Copyright © 2017

*For more information on The Life Book Movement please go to:* **www.thelifebook.com**

The Life Book Movement helps church youth leaders mobilize their students to give the gift of the Gospel to their peers.

Funded By

The Gideons International

# WHAT IS LIFE ABOUT?

## THE LIFE BOOK
### The Gospel of Mark

twitter.com/thelifebook
facebook.com/thelifebookofficial

# MY NOTES

# WHAT'S IN THE LIFE BOOK?

## ACT 1

Act 1 is God's story before Jesus shows up on the scene. It's a quick recap of the first part of the Bible before Jesus arrives. It explains how things were great, then went bad and why Jesus has to come make things right.

## ACT 2

Act 2 is straight from the book of Mark in the Bible. It's a first-hand account of the life of Jesus on earth. He does some amazing stuff.

## WHAT ABOUT YOU?

This part is about what God's story means for your life. What does Jesus have to do with you? What is your role in the world God created? What does God want from you?

## HELP!

This part gives some help with things you or your friends might be struggling with. The Bible is full of God's guidance for tough stuff in life. He made everything, so you can trust He knows what's best.

# STUDENT NOTES

Four students make notes and ask questions all through The Life Book.
(Free Clue: You can tell each student apart by their handwriting.)

## EMMIE

I just turned 15, love theater and want to be an actress someday, but I'm probably not good enough. My brother Austin is into all the God stuff. Me, not so much. But he's about the only good guy I know. Every guy I open up to acts like he loves me until he finds someone better. Maybe it's just me. Austin says God's not like that. We'll see.

## JB

Geek and proud of it. For a career, I think it'd be awesome to invent wireless electricity or find a way to use lasers to find oil beneath the ground. My geek crew and I are into science fiction, superhero stuff, RPGs and different strategy games. Favorite subjects are definitely science and math. Not sure how God fits into that. Not sure I can believe something I can't see or prove.

## TAYDEN

God ambushed me last year. My granddad took me fishing and talked to me about my sin and my need for forgiveness and salvation. It was like God opened my eyes. I was blind but now I could see. I saw my sin like never before, cried out to God for forgiveness and was born again in his little fishing boat. Nothing's been the same since. I'm graduating soon and I think God might be calling me to be a pastor. Whatever He wants, I'm good with it.

A bunch of people know I'm an orphan, but I'm not a wild child now like I used to be. My parents had me young and got addicted to drugs. So, yeah, I've been in foster homes most of my life. Tons of different schools. My current foster mom keeps me out of trouble. She's a christian. I don't know if I can become one with all the stuff I've done but I'd love to be like her.

# ADULT NOTES

MR. B

Tayden's my grandson and I met the rest of the kids at school where I work as a janitor. It's a dirty job, but someone has to do it. (I love dumb jokes.) God put me in their school. I believe that in my bones. Being a janitor wasn't my dream job after I left the Army, but if I can help people meet Jesus, I'll scrub toilets and mop floors any day. My heart breaks for young people today. They seem so lost. They need Jesus. I'm old, gray, and a bit slower than I used to be, but my passion for God still burns hot. I am a born again child of God and I want everyone to know my Heavenly Father like I do.

# ACT 1

## THE STORY OF GOD AND PEOPLE
(quick retelling of the first part of the Bible)

# GOD SPEAKS & EVERYTHING APPEARS

(check out Genesis 1)

God speaks and the entire universe shows up. With a few words,
He made the skies, the seas, the earth, the animals, and us. He
didn't have to create a world or us, but He chose to.

*That's crazy! He just spoke and everything showed up. - Emmie*

So who made God? No one. The Bible says He always was and
always will be. Don't worry, no one else really understands it
either. But when you're God, you don't have to explain yourself.

*Seems convenient. - j8*

# GOOD STUFF

(check out Genesis 2)

God speaks, everything shows up and He says all of it is good.
From gargantuan galaxies more beautiful and massive than we
can imagine to the simplicity of an amoeba, God says every little
bit is good.

The Bible says God made Adam and Eve, and all of us in His image. We may not be all-wise and all-powerful, but we are like Him
in some ways. He created us with the ability to love and laugh,
hope and dream, create and invent. He's not just an uncaring
creator looking on from a distance, He actually cares about the
people He made.

*This is cool. - Bella*

So God puts Adam and Eve in the Garden of Eden and gives them everything they could ever need. At this time, there was no death, no sin, no pain, no sorrow at all. It was a perfect world. Imagine God and mankind in the best, most trusting, most perfect relationship ever. God offered them everything of Himself and His creation, except for the fruit of one tree.

## SLIPPERY SERPENT

(check out Genesis 3)

Satan (a.k.a. the devil, old scratch, the evil one) shows up in the form of a talking snake. Who is satan? Believe it or not, he was an angel who was kicked out of heaven when he tried to take over—bad move. The serpent (satan in his snake disguise) tells Adam and Eve that God is lying to them, keeping things from them and they shouldn't trust Him. Turns out he's the big liar!

Satan said God was keeping the fruit of the tree from them because He didn't want them to be like Him. He also said God was lying about punishing them with death if they ate the fruit. Of course, Adam and Eve would trust God and not some slippery serpent, right?

They thought it over, ditched their Creator, chose to trust the snake Satan, and took a bite that would change the entire world. With one bite, trust was shattered; <u>the relationship between God and humans was broken, and evil (sin) entered into the perfect</u> world.

*Really? I didn't bite it. Why should I have to pay? —JB*

## THE CURSE ENTERS

A curse, just like in fairy tales — but real — crashed down on Adam and Eve and the entire human race that would come after them. The perfect world was now infected with the curse of sin. Now the perfect world would be messy and full of struggle, pain, suffering and shame.

Adam and Eve were kicked out of the perfect Garden. God could no longer walk with them, talk with them or be with them. Sin was now like a huge chasm separating God from humans. The close relationship disappeared as the evil sin virus saturated the world and separated it from God.

*Didn't think my sin was such a big deal. —Bella*

## THE CURSE LIVES

The curse comes to life as Adam and Eve's son Cain kills his brother Abel. Sin and evil spreads throughout the entire earth. Humans, infected by the curse, choose evil and reject God. Finally, God says enough is enough and orders a fresh start.

## DO-OVER

God found one righteous man and chose him to start everything all over. He asked Noah to build a huge boat to survive a world-wide flood. In this huge boat, Noah took his family and a pair of each type of animal so they could repopulate the earth. The ginormous flood came and everything was wiped out , except for the people and animals on the boat.

*I learned that the flood explains fossils and how things like the Grand Canyon formed so quickly. -Tayden*

# STARTING AGAIN

Because the flood didn't break the curse, sin and rebellion against God began again. God promised a man named Abraham that he would be the father of a new nation, a people belonging to God. His wife Sarah got pregnant when she was 90 years old and the promise began to be fulfilled.

Isaac (Abraham and Sarah's son) had a son named Jacob (who was quite a schemer), who moved his family to Egypt to escape a famine and to be with his son named Joseph. Even though Joseph went through a bunch of bad stuff like slavery and prison, he stayed faithful to God and eventually saved his whole family.

## SLAVERY

For about 400 years, God's people lived as slaves in Egypt. Until . . . God signed up Moses as the next leader by speaking to him through a burning bush (the bush was on fire, but not burning up) in the desert. Moses asked Pharaoh to set God's people free from slavery. He refused and God began sending nasty plagues. Still refusing, God finally sent the worst plague of all.

## PASSING OVER

Before God sent the last plague (death of the firstborn son from every family), He told Moses how to save the lives of His people. (God always seems to provide a way to be saved from terrible consequences.) Each family was to kill a lamb and smear the lamb's blood over the top of the door to their house.

God always provides a way.
— Tayden

Weird.
— Emmie

When the plague came, the firstborn son of each Egyptian family died, but all of God's people were saved. Finally, Pharoah set God's people free. After they left, he quickly changed his mind and followed them. With the Red Sea in front of them and Pharaoh's army behind them, God miraculously parted the sea and His people crossed over to freedom.

would've been cool to see
— BELLA

## 10 LAWS

Free from slavery, God gave Moses 10 laws designed to help the people get along with each other and relate to their Creator. But, the curse of sin was still in place. God's people did their own thing, turning to idols and making up other gods. The 10 laws couldn't rid the world of the curse.

*And we've been slaves to these supposed laws ever since — JB*

## BLOOD PAYMENT

As people continued to rebel against God's laws, He gave them a plan to pay for their law breaking. Because blood is the source of life, God's plan for payment involved the spilling of blood (like when He protected His people from the final plague in Egypt by using blood).

Animals were to be sacrificed as payment for sin. Though the curse could not be broken by these sacrifices, the shed blood of an animal would provide temporary cover from God's punishment of their sin.

*So animal blood made up for sin. Now I get the whole thing about Jesus shedding his blood. Makes more sense. -Tayden*

## THE PROMISE

Through His chosen prophets, God began to share the promise of one who would come and break the curse once and for all. A Messiah, a Savior was coming who would fix the relationship between mankind and God. This Savior would not only show us a new way to live, but He would also be the final sacrifice — his blood paying the final penalty for sin.

## JESUS APPEARS ON THE SCENE

In Act 2, Jesus appears on the scene as the eternal Son of God to break the curse of sin. His own people (God's chosen people) rejected Him. He lived a perfect life without sin and became the perfect sacrifice.

He died in our place and for our sin, drinking the cup of God's wrath and spilling His own blood as the final sacrifice to break the curse.

*I remember when God opened my eyes to this. Nothing's been the same since. — Jayden*

Then it happened...as miraculous proof that He was God's Son, God raised Jesus from the dead.

Here is the true story of Jesus that forever changed the world and just may change your life forever . . .

# ACT 2

BOOK OF MARK
(from the Bible)

# CHAPTER 1

## John the Baptist Prepares the Way

The beginning of the gospel of Jesus Christ, the Son of God.

As it is written in Isaiah the prophet,

*I think I've only had bad messengers. – BELLA*

> "Behold, I send my messenger before your face,
> who will prepare your way,
>     the voice of one crying in the wilderness:
> 'Prepare the way of the Lord,
>     make his paths straight,'"

John appeared, baptizing in the wilderness and proclaiming a baptism of repentance for the forgiveness of sins. And all the country of Judea and all Jerusalem were going out to him and were being baptized by him in the river Jordan, confessing their sins. Now John was clothed with camel's hair and wore a leather belt around his waist and ate locusts and wild honey. And he preached, saying, "After me comes he who is mightier than I, the strap of whose sandals I am not worthy to stoop down and untie. I have baptized you with water, but he will baptize you with the Holy Spirit."

*Locusts? Totally nasty! – Emmie*

*My sister goes to a church that talks about Holy Spirit baptism stuff. – JB*

### The Baptism of Jesus

In those days Jesus came from Nazareth of Galilee and was baptized by John in the Jordan. And when he came up out of the water, immediately he saw the heavens being torn open and the Spirit descending on him like a dove. And a voice came from heaven, "You are my beloved Son; with you I am well pleased."

*Would be nice to hear. — BELLA*

### The Temptation of Jesus

The Spirit immediately drove him out into the wilderness. And he was in the wilderness forty days, being tempted by Satan. And he was with the wild animals, and the angels were ministering to him.

*Angels serving me... I'm for that. JB*

### Jesus Begins His Ministry

Now after John was arrested, Jesus came into Galilee, proclaiming the gospel of God, and saying, "The time is fulfilled, and the kingdom of God is at hand; repent and believe in the gospel."

*Seems like churches don't say repent much anymore. — Tayden*

### Jesus Calls the First Disciples

Passing alongside the Sea of Galilee, he saw Simon and Andrew the brother of Simon casting a net into the sea, for they were fishermen. And Jesus said to them, "Follow me, and I will make you become fishers of men." And immediately they left their nets and followed him. And going on a little farther, he saw James the son of Zebedee and John his brother, who were in their boat mending the nets. And immediately he called them, and they left their father Zebedee in the boat with the hired servants and followed him.

*So they just left their jobs? How'd they get $$? —Emmie*

*Ditched their dad - my dad ditched me — BELLA*

## Jesus Heals a Man with an Unclean Spirit

And they went into Capernaum, and immediately on the Sabbath he entered the synagogue and was teaching. And they were astonished at his teaching, for he taught them as one who had authority, and not as the scribes. And immediately there was in their synagogue a man with an unclean spirit. And he cried out, "What have you to do with us, Jesus of Nazareth? Have you come to destroy us? I know who you are—the Holy One of God." But Jesus rebuked him, saying, "Be silent, and come out of him!" And the unclean spirit, convulsing him and crying out with a loud voice, came out of him. And they were all amazed, so that they questioned among themselves, saying, "What is this? A new teaching with authority! He commands even the unclean spirits, and they obey him." And at once his fame spread everywhere throughout all the surrounding region of Galilee.

*How was it different? —JB*

*So demons knew who he was but no one else did? — JB*

*Dude! He shut him down. —Jayden*

## Jesus Heals Many

And immediately he left the synagogue and entered the house of
Simon and Andrew, with James and John. Now Simon's mother-
in-law lay ill with a fever, and immediately they told him about
her. And he came and took her by the hand and lifted her up, and
the fever left her, and she began to serve them.

*That's cool
- Emmie*

That evening at sundown they brought to him all who were sick or
oppressed by demons. And the whole city was gathered together
at the door. And he healed many who were sick with various
diseases, and cast out many demons. And he would not permit
the demons to speak, because they knew him.

*Totally went
viral
- Emmie*

*Ha.... Shut up
demons! Nice. -JB*

## Jesus Preaches in Galilee

And rising very early in the morning, while it was still dark, he
departed and went out to a desolate place, and there he prayed.
And Simon and those who were with him searched for him, and
they found him and said to him, "Everyone is looking for you."
And he said to them, "Let us go on to the next towns, that I
may preach there also, for that is why I came out." And he went
throughout all Galilee, preaching in their synagogues and casting
out demons.

*My foster
mother does
this every
morning.
- BELLA*

## Jesus Cleanses a Leper

And a leper came to him, imploring him, and kneeling said to him, "If you will, you can make me clean." Moved with pity, he stretched out his hand and touched him and said to him, "I will; be clean." And immediately the leprosy left him, and he was made clean. And Jesus sternly charged him and sent him away at once, and said to him, "See that you say nothing to anyone, but go, show yourself to the priest and offer for your cleansing what Moses commanded, for a proof to them." But he went out and began to talk freely about it, and to spread the news, so that Jesus could no longer openly enter a town, but was out in desolate places, and people were coming to him from every quarter.

*He kind of seems like a carring guy.*
*- Emmie*

*If God fixed my situation, I couldn't shut up about it. - BELLA*

# CHAPTER 2
## Jesus Heals a Paralytic

And when he returned to Capernaum after some days, it was reported that he was at home. And many were gathered together, so that there was no more room, not even at the door. And he was preaching the word to them. And they came, bringing to him a paralytic carried by four men. And when they could not get near him because of the crowd, they removed the roof above him, and when they had made an opening, they let down the bed on which

*I have to admit this is pretty cool. Cutting a hole in the roof. What if it rains? - JB*

the paralytic lay. And when Jesus saw their faith, he said to the paralytic, "Son, your sins are forgiven." Now some of the scribes were sitting there, questioning in their hearts, "Why does this man speak like that? He is blaspheming! Who can forgive sins but God alone?" And immediately Jesus, perceiving in his spirit that they thus questioned within themselves, said to them, "Why do you question these things in your hearts? Which is easier, to say to the paralytic, 'Your sins are forgiven,' or to say, 'Rise, take up your bed and walk'? But that you may know that the Son of Man has authority on earth to forgive sins"—he said to the paralytic— "I say to you, rise, pick up your bed, and go home." And he rose and immediately picked up his bed and went out before them all, so that they were all amazed and glorified God, saying, "We never saw anything like this!"

### Jesus Calls Levi

He went out again beside the sea, and all the crowd was coming to him, and he was teaching them. And as he passed by, he saw Levi the son of Alphaeus sitting at the tax booth, and he said to him, "Follow me." And he rose and followed him.

And as he reclined at table in his house, many tax collectors and sinners were reclining with Jesus and his disciples, for there were many who followed him. And the scribes of the Pharisees, when they saw that he was eating with sinners and tax collectors, said to his disciples, "Why does he eat with tax collectors and sinners?" And when Jesus heard it, he said to them, "Those who are well have no need of a physician, but those who are sick. I came not to call the righteous, but sinners."

*confused.. – BELLA*

## A Question About Fasting

Now John's disciples and the Pharisees were fasting. And people came and said to him, "Why do John's disciples and the disciples of the Pharisees fast, but your disciples do not fast?" And Jesus said to them, "Can the wedding guests fast while the bridegroom is with them? As long as they have the bridegroom with them, they cannot fast. The days will come when the bridegroom is taken away from them, and then they will fast in that day. No one sews a piece of unshrunk cloth on an old garment. If he does, the patch tears away from it, the new from the old, and a worse tear is made. And no one puts new wine into old wineskins. If he does, the wine will burst the skins—and the wine is destroyed, and so are the skins. But new wine is for fresh wineskins."

*We did a 30-hour fast thing at our church. –Tayden*

### Jesus Is Lord of the Sabbath

One Sabbath he was going through the grainfields, and as they made their way, his disciples began to pluck heads of grain. And the Pharisees were saying to him, "Look, why are they doing what is not lawful on the Sabbath?" And he said to them, "Have you never read what David did, when he was in need and was hungry, he and those who were with him: how he entered the house of God, in the time of Abiathar the high priest, and ate the bread of the Presence, which it is not lawful for any but the priests to eat, and also gave it to those who were with him?" And he said to them, "The Sabbath was made for man, not man for the Sabbath. So the Son of Man is lord even of the Sabbath."

*They don't seem to like him. - Emmie*

*I'm down with a day off. -JB*

## CHAPTER 3
### A Man with a Withered Hand

Again he entered the synagogue, and a man was there with a withered hand. And they watched Jesus, to see whether he would heal him on the Sabbath, so that they might accuse him. And he said to the man with the withered hand, "Come here." And he said to them, "Is it lawful on the Sabbath to do good or to do harm, to save life or to kill?" But they were silent. And he looked around at them with anger, grieved at their hardness of heart, and said to the man, "Stretch out your hand." He stretched it

*I know idiots like these guys - Emmie*

out, and his hand was restored. The Pharisees went out and immediately held counsel with the Herodians against him, how to destroy him.

*I'd wanna check out what He's doing too.*
*– BELLA*

## A Great Crowd Follows Jesus

Jesus withdrew with his disciples to the sea, and a great crowd followed, from Galilee and Judea and Jerusalem and Idumea and from beyond the Jordan and from around Tyre and Sidon. When the great crowd heard all that he was doing, they came to him. And he told his disciples to have a boat ready for him because of the crowd, lest they crush him, for he had healed many, so that all who had diseases pressed around him to touch him. And whenever the unclean spirits saw him, they fell down before him and cried out, "You are the Son of God." And he strictly ordered them not to make him known.

*Nice – his own security crew.*
*–Tayden*

*Again...demons knew who Jesus was, but these religious people didn't? – JB*

## The Twelve Apostles

And he went up on the mountain and called to him those whom he desired, and they came to him. And he appointed twelve (whom he also named apostles) so that they might be with him and he might send them out to preach and have authority to cast out demons. He appointed the twelve: Simon (to whom he gave

*I'm in.*
*–Tayden*

the name Peter); James the son of Zebedee and John the brother of James (to whom he gave the name Boanerges, that is, Sons of Thunder); Andrew, and Philip, and Bartholomew, and Matthew, and Thomas, and James the son of Alphaeus, and Thaddaeus, and Simon the Zealot, and Judas Iscariot, who betrayed him.

Then he went home, and the crowd gathered again, so that they could not even eat. And when his family heard it, they went out to seize him, for they were saying, "He is out of his mind."

*That's what people said about my brother when he became a Christian. —Emmie*

### Blasphemy Against the Holy Spirit
And the scribes who came down from Jerusalem were saying, "He is possessed by Beelzebul," and "by the prince of demons he casts out the demons." And he called them to him and said to them in parables, "How can Satan cast out Satan? If a kingdom is divided against itself, that kingdom cannot stand. And if a house is divided against itself, that house will not be able to stand. And if Satan has risen up against himself and is divided, he cannot stand, but is coming to an end. But no one can enter a strong man's house and plunder his goods, unless he first binds the strong man. Then indeed he may plunder his house.

*Makes sense. —JB*

"Truly, I say to you, all sins will be forgiven the children of man, and whatever blasphemies they utter, but whoever blasphemes against the Holy Spirit never has forgiveness, but is guilty of an eternal sin"— for they were saying, "He has an unclean spirit."

*What is this eternal sin? —BELLA* ✱

*Honestly Bella, I'm not totally sure. But I do know that Jesus died so that you and I could be forgiven — Mr. B*

### Jesus' Mother and Brothers

And his mother and his brothers came, and standing outside they sent to him and called him. And a crowd was sitting around him, and they said to him, "Your mother and your brothers are outside, seeking you." And he answered them, "Who are my mother and my brothers?" And looking about at those who sat around him, he said, "Here are my mother and my brothers! For whoever does the will of God, he is my brother and sister and mother."

*sounds like my life —BELLA*

*It's only been 6 months, but my foster mom is already more of a mom than I've ever had. —BELLA*

## CHAPTER 4

### The Parable of the Sower

Again he began to teach beside the sea. And a very large crowd gathered about him, so that he got into a boat and sat in it on the sea, and the whole crowd was beside the sea on the land. And he was teaching them many things in parables, and in his teaching he said to them: "Listen! Behold, a sower went out to sow. And as he sowed, some seed fell along the path, and the birds came and devoured it. Other seed fell on rocky ground, where it did not have much soil, and immediately it sprang up, since it had no depth of soil. And when the sun rose, it was scorched, and since it had no root, it withered away. Other seed fell among thorns, and the thorns grew up and choked it, and it yielded no grain. And other seeds fell into good soil and produced grain, growing up and increasing and yielding thirtyfold and sixtyfold and a hundredfold." **And he said,** "He who has ears to hear, let him hear."

### The Purpose of the Parables

And when he was alone, those around him with the twelve asked him about the parables. And he said to them, "To you has been given the secret of the kingdom of God, but for those outside everything is in parables, so that

*Jesus didn't want people to understand???*
*- Emmie*

"'they may indeed see but not perceive,
and may indeed hear but not understand,
lest they should turn and be forgiven.'"

And he said to them, "Do you not understand this parable? How then will you understand all the parables? The sower sows the word. And these are the ones along the path, where the word is sown: when they hear, Satan immediately comes and takes away the word that is sown in them. And these are the ones sown on rocky ground: the ones who, when they hear the word, immediately receive it with joy. And they have no root in themselves, but endure for a while; then, when tribulation or persecution arises on account of the word, <u>immediately they fall away.</u> And others are the ones sown among thorns. They are those who hear the word, but the cares of the world and the <u>deceitfulness of riches</u> and the desires for other things enter in and choke the word, and it proves unfruitful. But those that were sown on the good soil are the ones who hear the word and accept it and bear fruit, thirtyfold and sixtyfold and a hundredfold."

*My brother is a good soil one.*

*– Emmie*

*I've seen this. People get all religious for a few months, then it passes. So fake! –J8*

*I have to be careful with this. –Tayden*

## A Lamp Under a Basket

And he said to them, "Is a lamp brought in to be put under a basket, or under a bed, and not on a stand? For nothing is hidden except to be made manifest; nor is anything secret except to come to light. If anyone has ears to hear, let him hear." And he said to them, "Pay attention to what you hear: with the measure you use, it will be measured to you, and still more will be added to you. For to the one who has, more will be given, and from the one who has not, even what he has will be taken away."

*I don't have much anyway. –Bella*

## The Parable of the Seed Growing

And he said, "The kingdom of God is as if a man should scatter seed on the ground. He sleeps and rises night and day, and the seed sprouts and grows; he knows not how. The earth produces by itself, first the blade, then the ear, then the full grain in the ear. But when the grain is ripe, at once he puts in the sickle, because the harvest has come."  *God does all the work.  -Tayden*

### The Parable of the Mustard Seed

And he said, "With what can we compare the kingdom of God, or what parable shall we use for it? It is like a grain of mustard seed, which, when sown on the ground, is the smallest of all the seeds on earth, yet when it is sown it grows up and becomes larger than all the garden plants and puts out large branches, so that the birds of the air can make nests in its shade."

*I'm really small too. :) -Emmie*

With many such parables he spoke the word to them, as they were able to hear it. He did not speak to them without a parable, but privately to his own disciples he explained everything.

*I still don't understand why this is secret. -Emmie*

### Jesus Calms a Storm

On that day, when evening had come, he said to them, "Let us go across to the other side." And leaving the crowd, they took him with them in the boat, just as he was. And other boats were with him. And a great windstorm arose, and the waves were breaking into the boat, so that the boat was already filling. But he was in the stern, asleep on the cushion. And they woke him and said to him, "Teacher, do you not care that we are perishing?" And he awoke and rebuked the wind and said to the sea, "Peace! Be still!" And the wind ceased, and there was a great calm. He said to them, "Why are you so afraid? Have you still no faith?" And they were filled with great fear and said to one another, "Who then is this, that even the wind and the sea obey him?"

*I might believe if I saw that. —JB*

## CHAPTER 5
### Jesus Heals a Man with a Demon

They came to the other side of the sea, to the country of the Gerasenes. And when Jesus had stepped out of the boat, immediately there met him out of the tombs a man with an unclean spirit. He lived among the tombs. And no one could bind him anymore, not even with a chain, for he had often been bound with shackles and chains, but he wrenched the chains apart, and he broke the shackles in pieces. No one had the strength to subdue him. Night and day among the tombs and on the mountains he was always crying out and cutting himself with stones. And when he saw Jesus from afar, he ran and fell down before him. And crying out with a loud voice, he said,

*MMA Champ? —Tayden*

*I used to cut. —Bella*

"What have you to do with me, Jesus, Son of the Most High God? I adjure you by God, do not torment me." For he was saying to him, "Come out of the man, you unclean spirit!" And Jesus asked him, "What is your name?" He replied, "My name is Legion, for we are many." And he begged him earnestly not to send them out of the country. Now a great herd of pigs was feeding there on the hillside, and they begged him, saying, "Send us to the pigs; let us enter them." So he gave them permission. And the unclean spirits came out and entered the pigs; and the herd, numbering about two thousand, rushed down the steep bank into the sea and drowned in the sea.

The herdsmen fled and told it in the city and in the country. And people came to see what it was that had happened. And they came to Jesus and saw the demon-possessed man, the one who had had the legion, sitting there, clothed and in his right mind, and they were afraid. And those who had seen it described to them what had happened to the demon-possessed man and to the pigs. And they began to beg Jesus to depart from their region. As he was getting into the boat, the man who had been possessed with demons begged him that he might be with him. And he did not permit him but said to him, "Go home to your friends and tell them how much the Lord has done for you, and how he has had mercy on you." And he went away and began to proclaim in the Decapolis how much Jesus had done for him, and everyone marveled.

*I like the way Jesus tells messed up people to tell others about Him. -Bella*

## Jesus Heals a Woman and Jairus's Daughter

And when Jesus had crossed again in the boat to the other side, a great crowd gathered about him, and he was beside the sea. Then came one of the rulers of the synagogue, Jairus by name, and seeing him, he fell at his feet and implored him earnestly, saying, "My little daughter is at the point of death. Come and lay your hands on her, so that she may be made well and live." And he went with him.

And a great crowd followed him and thronged about him. And there was a woman who had had a discharge of blood for twelve years, and who had suffered much under many physicians, and had spent all that she had, and was no better but rather grew worse. She had heard the reports about Jesus and came up behind him in the crowd and touched his garment. For she said, "If I touch even his garments, I will be made well." And immediately the flow of blood dried up, and she felt in her body that she was healed of her disease. And Jesus, perceiving in himself that <u>power had gone out from him</u>, immediately turned

*Maybe if I touched his robe I could have magically been born into a real family. -Bella*

*Seriously? How could he know? -JB*

*He's God dude! -Tayden*

about in the crowd and said, "Who touched my garments?" And his disciples said to him, "You see the crowd pressing around you, and yet you say, 'Who touched me?'" And he looked around to see who had done it. But the woman, knowing what had happened to her, came in fear and trembling and fell down before him and told him the whole truth. And he said to her, "Daughter, your faith has made you well; go in peace, and be healed of your disease."

*Wish he'd call me daughter.*
*— BELLA*

While he was still speaking, there came from the ruler's house some who said, "Your daughter is dead. Why trouble the Teacher any further?" But overhearing what they said, Jesus said to the ruler of the synagogue, "Do not fear, only believe." And he allowed no one to follow him except Peter and James and John the brother of James. They came to the house of the ruler of the synagogue, and Jesus saw a commotion, people weeping and wailing loudly. And when he had entered, he said to them, "Why are you making a commotion and weeping? The child is not dead but sleeping." And they laughed at him. But he put them all outside and took the child's father and mother and those who were with him and went in where the child was. Taking her by the hand he said to her, "Talitha cumi," which means, "Little girl, I say to you, arise." And immediately the girl got up and

*That's what my brother keeps telling me.*
*— Emmie*

*They want to kill him. they ask him to leave. now they laugh at him. I thought everyone loved Jesus in the Bible.*
*—JB*

began walking (for she was twelve years of age), and they were immediately overcome with amazement. And he strictly charged them that no one should know this, and told them to give her something to eat.

*→ I still don't get why He keeps this stuff secret.*
*- Emmie*

# CHAPTER 6
## Jesus Rejected at Nazareth

He went away from there and came to his hometown, and his disciples followed him. And on the Sabbath he began to teach in the synagogue, and many who heard him were astonished, saying, "Where did this man get these things? What is the wisdom given to him? How are such mighty works done by his hands? Is not this the carpenter, the son of Mary and brother of James and Joses and Judas and Simon? And are not his sisters here with us?" And they took offense at him. And Jesus said to them, "A prophet is not without honor, except in his hometown and among his relatives and in his own household." And he could do no mighty work there, except that he laid his hands on a few sick people and healed them. And he marveled because of their unbelief.

*It's like they're bigots. They can't believe a local boy could be doing stuff like this.*
*-Tayden*

And he went about among the villages teaching.

*Me too! Just look at God's creation. How can you not believe?*
*- Tayden*

### Jesus Sends Out the Twelve Apostles

And he called the twelve and began to send them out two by two, and gave them authority over the unclean spirits. He charged them to take nothing for their journey except a staff—no bread, no bag, no money in their belts— but to wear sandals and not put on two tunics. And he said to them, "Whenever you enter a house, stay there until you depart from there. And if any place will not receive you and they will not listen to you, when you leave, shake off the dust that is on your feet as a testimony against them." So they went out and proclaimed that people should repent. And they cast out many demons and anointed with oil many who were sick and healed them.

*Traveling light. I'm into that. — Bella*

### The Death of John the Baptist

King Herod heard of it, for Jesus' name had become known. Some said, "John the Baptist has been raised from the dead. That is why these miraculous powers are at work in him." But others said, "He is Elijah." And others said, "He is a prophet, like one of the prophets of old." But when Herod heard of it, he said, "John, whom I beheaded, has been raised." For it was Herod who had sent and seized John and bound him in prison for the sake of Herodias, his brother Philip's wife, because he had married

*So again... demons knew who Jesus was, but these guys couldn't figure it out. Stupid or blind? — Emmie*

her. For John had been saying to Herod, "It is not lawful for you to have your brother's wife." And Herodias had a grudge against him and wanted to put him to death. But she could not, for Herod feared John, knowing that he was a righteous and holy man, and he kept him safe. When he heard him, he was greatly perplexed, and yet he heard him gladly.

But an opportunity came when Herod on his birthday gave a banquet for his nobles and military commanders and the leading men of Galilee. For when Herodias's daughter came in and danced, she pleased Herod and his guests. And the king said to the girl, "Ask me for whatever you wish, and I will give it to you." And he vowed to her, "Whatever you ask me, I will give you, up to half of my kingdom." And she went out and said to her mother, "For what should I ask?" And she said, "The head of John the Baptist." And she came in immediately with haste to the king and asked, saying, "I want you to give me at once the head of John the Baptist on a platter." And the king was exceedingly sorry, but because of his oaths and his guests he did not want to break his word to her. And immediately the king sent an executioner with orders to bring John's head. He went and beheaded him in the prison and brought his head on a platter and gave it to the girl, and the girl gave it to her mother. When his disciples heard of it,

SICK!!!
> - Emmie

they came and took his body and laid it in a tomb.

**Jesus Feeds the Five Thousand**

The apostles returned to Jesus and told him all that they had
done and taught. And he said to them, "Come away by yourselves
to a desolate place and rest a while." For many were coming
and going, and they had no leisure even to eat. And they went
away in the boat to a desolate place by themselves. Now many
saw them going and recognized them, and they ran there on
foot from all the towns and got there ahead of them. When he
went ashore he saw a great crowd, and he had compassion on
them, because they were like sheep without a shepherd. And
he began to teach them many things. And when it grew late, his
disciples came to him and said, "This is a desolate place, and
the hour is now late. Send them away to go into the surrounding
countryside and villages and buy themselves something to eat."
But he answered them, "You give them something to eat." And
they said to him, "Shall we go and buy two hundred denarii worth
of bread and give it to them to eat?" And he said to them, "How
many loaves do you have? Go and see." And when they had found
out, they said, "Five, and two fish." Then he commanded them
all to sit down in groups on the green grass. So they sat down in
groups, by hundreds and by fifties. And taking the five loaves

*I could use some serious rest. —JB*

*story of my life —Bella*

*I remember this story. Seems too good to be true. —JB*

and the two fish, he looked up to heaven and said a blessing and broke the loaves and gave them to the disciples to set before the people. And he divided the two fish among them all. And they all ate and were satisfied. And they took up twelve baskets full of broken pieces and of the fish. And those who ate the loaves were five thousand men. ＊ *God created everything. These miracles are easy for Him. — Mr. D*

## Jesus Walks on the Water

Immediately he made his disciples get into the boat and go before him to the other side, to Bethsaida, while he dismissed the crowd. And after he had taken leave of them, he went up on the mountain to pray. And when evening came, the boat was out on the sea, and he was alone on the land. And he saw that they were making headway painfully, for the wind was against them. And about the fourth watch of the night he came to them, walking on the sea. He meant to pass by them, but when they saw him walking on the sea they thought it was a ghost, and cried out, for they all saw him and were terrified. But immediately he spoke to them and said, "Take heart; it is I. Do not be afraid." And he got into the boat with them, and the wind ceased. And they were utterly astounded, for they did not understand about the loaves, but their hearts were hardened.

*AWESOME! — Emmie*

### Jesus Heals the Sick in Gennesaret

When they had crossed over, they came to land at Gennesaret and moored to the shore. And when they got out of the boat, the people immediately recognized him and ran about the whole region and began to bring the sick people on their beds to wherever they heard he was. And wherever he came, in villages, cities, or countryside, they laid the sick in the marketplaces and implored him that they might touch even the fringe of his garment. And as many as touched it were made well.

*Everyone who touched his tassel was healed. I want to believe this actually happened.*
*— Bella*

## CHAPTER 7
### Traditions and Commandments

Now when the Pharisees gathered to him, with some of the scribes who had come from Jerusalem, they saw that some of his disciples ate with hands that were defiled, that is, unwashed. (For the Pharisees and all the Jews do not eat unless they wash their hands properly, holding to the tradition of the elders, and when they come from the marketplace, they do not eat unless they wash. And there are many other traditions that they observe, such as the washing of cups and pots and copper vessels and dining couches.) And the Pharisees and the scribes asked him, "Why do your disciples not walk according to the

*My mom always has hand sanitizer with her.*
*— Tayden*

tradition of the elders, but eat with defiled hands?" And he said to them, "Well did Isaiah prophesy of you hypocrites, as it is written,

*I didn't know Jesus was a trash talker. — Tayden*

> "'This people honors me with their lips,
>> but their heart is far from me;
>> in vain do they worship me,
>>> teaching as doctrines the commandments of men.'

*I know Christians like this. All talk and totally caught up in tradition. — JB*

You leave the commandment of God and hold to the tradition of men."

And he said to them, "You have a fine way of rejecting the commandment of God in order to establish your tradition! For Moses said, 'Honor your father and your mother'; and, 'Whoever reviles father or mother must surely die.' But you say, 'If a man tells his father or his mother, "Whatever you would have gained from me is Corban"' (that is, given to God)— then you no longer permit him to do anything for his father or mother, thus making void the word of God by your tradition that you have handed down. And many such things you do."

*Not sure what He's talking about here. — Emmie*

## What Defiles a Person

And he called the people to him again and said to them, "Hear me, all of you, and understand: There is nothing outside a person that by going into him can defile him, but the things that come out of a person are what defile him." And when he had entered the house and left the people, his disciples asked him about the parable. And he said to them, "Then are you also without understanding? Do you not see that whatever goes into a person from outside cannot defile him, since it enters not his heart but his stomach, and is expelled?" (Thus he declared all foods clean.) And he said, "What comes out of a person is what defiles him. For from within, out of the heart of man, come evil thoughts, sexual immorality, theft, murder, adultery, coveting, wickedness, deceit, sensuality, envy, slander, pride, foolishness. All these evil things come from within, and they defile a person."

*Kind of makes more sense now... maybe. Emmie*

## The Syrophoenician Woman's Faith

And from there he arose and went away to the region of Tyre and Sidon. And he entered a house and did not want anyone to know, yet he could not be hidden. But immediately a woman whose little daughter had an unclean spirit heard of him and came and fell down at his feet. Now the woman was a Gentile, a Syrophoenician by birth. And she begged him to cast the demon out of her daughter. And he said to her, "Let the children be fed

*Jesus going ninja style. - Tayden*

first, for it is not right to take the children's bread and throw it to the dogs." But she answered him, "Yes, Lord; yet even the dogs under the table eat the children's crumbs." And he said to her, "For this statement you may go your way; the demon has left your daughter." And she went home and found the child lying in bed and the demon gone. *Seems like Jesus plays games with people. — JB*

## Jesus Heals a Deaf Man

Then he returned from the region of Tyre and went through Sidon to the Sea of Galilee, in the region of the Decapolis. And they brought to him a man who was deaf and had a speech impediment, and they begged him to lay his hand on him. And taking him aside from the crowd privately, he put his fingers into his ears, and after spitting touched his tongue. And looking up *NASTY! — BELLA* to heaven, he sighed and said to him, "Ephphatha," that is, "Be opened." And his ears were opened, his tongue was released, and he spoke plainly. And Jesus charged them to tell no one. But the more he charged them, the more zealously they proclaimed it. And they were astonished beyond measure, saying, "He has done all things well. He even makes the deaf hear and the mute speak."

*One family I stayed with had a deaf kid so I learned some sign language. — BELLA*

## CHAPTER 8
### Jesus Feeds the Four Thousand

In those days, when again a great crowd had gathered, and they had nothing to eat, he called his disciples to him and said to them, "I have compassion on the crowd, because they have been with me now three days and have nothing to eat. And if I send them away hungry to their homes, they will faint on the way. And some of them have come from far away." And his disciples answered him, "How can one feed these people with bread here in this desolate place?" And he asked them, "How many loaves do you have?" They said, "Seven." And he directed the crowd to sit down on the ground. And he took the seven loaves, and having given thanks, he broke them and gave them to his disciples to set before the people; and they set them before the crowd. And they had a few small fish. And having blessed them, he said that these also should be set before them. And they ate and were satisfied. And they took up the broken pieces left over, seven baskets full. And there were about four thousand people. And he sent them away. And immediately he got into the boat with his disciples and went to the district of Dalmanutha.

*Jesus takes a little and makes a ton. - Tayden*

### The Pharisees Demand a Sign

*Jesus sighed? - Emmie*

The Pharisees came and began to argue with him, seeking from him a sign from heaven to test him. And he sighed deeply in his spirit and said, "Why does this generation seek a sign? Truly, I say to you, no sign will be given to this generation." And he left them, got into the boat again, and went to the other side.

### The Leaven of the Pharisees and Herod

Now they had forgotten to bring bread, and they had only one loaf with them in the boat. And he cautioned them, saying, "Watch out; beware of the leaven of the Pharisees and the leaven of Herod." And they began discussing with one another the fact *Jesus gets ticked off. — Emmie* that they had no bread. And Jesus, aware of this, said to them, "Why are you discussing the fact that you have no bread? Do you not yet perceive or understand? Are your hearts hardened? Having eyes do you not see, and having ears do you not hear? And do you not remember? When I broke the five loaves for the five thousand, how many baskets full of broken pieces did you take up?" They said to him, "Twelve." "And the seven for the four thousand, how many baskets full of broken pieces did you take up?" And they said to him, "Seven." And he said to them, "Do you not yet understand?" *No, I don't. — JB*

### Jesus Heals a Blind Man at Bethsaida

And they came to Bethsaida. And some people brought to him a blind man and begged him to touch him. And he took the blind man by the hand and led him out of the village, and when he had spit on his eyes and laid his hands on him, he asked him, "Do you see anything?" And he looked up and said, "I see people, but they look like trees, walking." Then Jesus laid his hands on his eyes again; and he opened his eyes, his sight was restored, and he saw everything clearly. And he sent him to his home, saying, "Do not even enter the village." ⟶

### Peter Confesses Jesus as the Christ

And Jesus went on with his disciples to the villages of Caesarea Philippi. And on the way he asked his disciples, "Who do people say that I am?" And they told him, "John the Baptist; and others say, Elijah; and others, one of the prophets." And he asked them, "But who do you say that I am?" Peter answered him, "You are the Christ." And he strictly charged them to tell no one about him.

### Jesus Foretells His Death and Resurrection

And he began to teach them that the Son of Man must suffer many things and be rejected by the elders and the chief priests and the scribes and be killed, and after three days rise again. And he said this plainly. And Peter took him aside and began to rebuke him.* But turning and seeing his disciples, he rebuked Peter and said, "Get behind me, Satan! For you are not setting your mind on the things of God, but on the things of man."

*Jesus is lil up!* — Tayden

And calling the crowd to him with his disciples, he said to them, "If anyone would come after me, let him deny himself and take up his cross and follow me. For whoever would save his life will lose it, but whoever loses his life for my sake and the gospel's will save it. For what does it profit a man to gain the whole world and forfeit his soul? For what can a man give in return for his soul? For whoever is ashamed of me and of my words in this adulterous and sinful generation, of him will the Son of Man also be ashamed when he comes in the glory of his Father with the holy angels."

*I couldn't imagine even thinking about "rebuking" Jesus. Peter must have been pretty arrogant.* — Mr. B

# CHAPTER 9

And he said to them, "Truly, I say to you, there are some standing here who will not taste death until they see the kingdom of God after it has come with power."

*"Hmmm..."* — JB

### The Transfiguration

And after six days Jesus took with him Peter and James and John, and led them up a high mountain by themselves. And he was transfigured before them, and his clothes became radiant, intensely white, as no one on earth could bleach them. And there appeared to them Elijah with Moses, and they were talking with Jesus. And Peter said to Jesus, "Rabbi, it is good that we are here. Let us make three tents, one for you and one for Moses and one for Elijah." For he did not know what to say, for they were terrified. And a cloud overshadowed them, and a voice came out of the cloud, "This is my beloved Son; listen to him." And suddenly, looking around, they no longer saw anyone with them but Jesus only. *So, let's put up some tents? Strange reaction.* — JB

And as they were coming down the mountain, he charged them to tell no one what they had seen, until the Son of Man had risen from the dead. So they kept the matter to themselves, questioning what this rising from the dead might mean. And they asked him, "Why do the scribes say that first Elijah must come?" And he said to them, "Elijah does come first to restore all things. And how is it written of the Son of Man that he should suffer many things and be treated with contempt? But I tell you that Elijah has come, and they did to him whatever they pleased, as it is written of him." *Actually the Old Testament prophecies that Jesus fulfilled are about the Messiah suffering.* — Tayden

## Jesus Heals a Boy with an Unclean Spirit

And when they came to the disciples, they saw a great crowd around them, and scribes arguing with them. And immediately all the crowd, when they saw him, were greatly amazed and ran up to him and greeted him. And he asked them, "What are you arguing about with them?" And someone from the crowd answered him, "Teacher, I brought my son to you, for he has a spirit that makes him mute. And whenever it seizes him, it throws him down, and he foams and grinds his teeth and becomes rigid. So I asked your disciples to cast it out, and they were not able." And he answered them, "O faithless generation, how long am I to be with you? How long am I to bear with you? Bring him to me." And they brought the boy to him. And when the spirit saw him, immediately it convulsed the boy, and he fell on the ground and rolled about, foaming at the mouth. And Jesus asked his father, "How long has this been happening to him?" And he said, "From childhood. And it has often cast him into fire and into water, to destroy him. But if you can do anything, have compassion on us and help us." And Jesus said to him, "'If you can'! All things are possible for one who believes." Immediately the father of the child cried out and said, "I believe; help my unbelief!" And when Jesus saw that a crowd came running together, he rebuked the unclean spirit, saying to it, "You mute and deaf spirit, I

*Ha! Jesus says let me handle it. I'd love it if he'd handle my problems. - Bella*

*Jesus doesn't do IF. -Tayden*

command you, come out of him and never enter him again." And after crying out and convulsing him terribly, it came out, and the boy was like a corpse, so that most of them said, "He is dead." But Jesus took him by the hand and lifted him up, and he arose. And when he had entered the house, his disciples asked him privately, "Why could we not cast it out?" And he said to them, "This kind cannot be driven out by anything but prayer."

*Freaky! - Bella*

*Different kinds of demon possession? -JB*

## Jesus Again Foretells Death, Resurrection

They went on from there and passed through Galilee. And he did not want anyone to know, for he was teaching his disciples, saying to them, "The Son of Man is going to be delivered into the hands of men, and they will kill him. And when he is killed, after three days he will rise." But they did not understand the saying, and were afraid to ask him.

*I might be afraid too. - Bella*

## Who Is the Greatest?

And they came to Capernaum. And when he was in the house he asked them, "What were you discussing on the way?" But they kept silent, for on the way they had argued with one another about who was the greatest. And he sat down and called the

*I want to believe like my brother does -Emmie*

twelve. And he said to them, "If anyone would be first, he must be last of all and servant of all." And he took a child and put him in the midst of them, and taking him in his arms, he said to them, "Whoever receives one such child in my name receives me, and whoever receives me, receives not me but him who sent me."

*Seems backwards. -JB*

## Anyone Not Against Us Is for Us

John said to him, "Teacher, we saw someone casting out demons in your name, and we tried to stop him, because he was not following us." But Jesus said, "Do not stop him, for no one who does a mighty work in my name will be able soon afterward to speak evil of me. For the one who is not against us is for us. For truly, I say to you, whoever gives you a cup of water to drink because you belong to Christ will by no means lose his reward.

*What about those guys who seem to do it for the $$? -JB*

## Temptations to Sin

"Whoever causes one of these little ones who believe in me to sin, it would be better for him if a great millstone were hung around his neck and he were thrown into the sea. And if your hand causes you to sin, cut it off. It is better for you to enter life crippled than with two hands to go to hell, to the unquenchable fire. And if your foot causes you to sin, cut it off. It is better for you to enter life lame than with two feet to be thrown into hell.

*I wouldn't have any body parts left! - bella*

HARSH!
-Tayden

And if your eye causes you to sin, tear it out It is better for you to enter the kingdom of God with one eye than with two eyes to be thrown into hell, 'where their worm does not die and the fire is not quenched.' For everyone will be salted with fire. Salt is good, but if the salt has lost its saltiness, how will you make it salty again? Have salt in yourselves, and be at peace with one another."

Because of God's grace, Jesus pays the penalty for all our sin and we don't have to cut anything off or gouge anything out. Without Jesus taking care of my sin I'd be eyeless and limbless too! — Mr. B

# CHAPTER 10
### Teaching About Divorce

And he left there and went to the region of Judea and beyond the Jordan, and crowds gathered to him again. And again, as was his custom, he taught them. And Pharisees came up and in order to test him asked, "Is it lawful for a man to divorce his wife?" He answered them, "What did Moses command you?" They said, "Moses allowed a man to write a certificate of divorce and to send her away." And Jesus said to them, "Because of your hardness of heart he wrote you this commandment. But from the beginning of creation, 'God made them male and female.' 'Therefore a man shall leave his father and mother and hold fast to his wife, and the two shall become one flesh.' So they

DIVORCE STINKS! Dad divorced mom when he left.
— BELLA

He never seems to answer them directly. — JB

are no longer two but one flesh. What therefore God has joined together, let not man separate."

And in the house the disciples asked him again about this matter. And he said to them, "Whoever divorces his wife and marries another commits adultery against her, and if she divorces her husband and marries another, she commits adultery."

*For married people, staying together for life is God's perfect plan. Divorce seems too easy today. My wife and I have had some terribly tough times, but somehow with God's help we stuck it out. I'm sure glad we did. - Mr. B*

*I know I want someone for life. - Tayden*

### Let the Children Come to Me

And they were bringing children to him that he might touch them, and the disciples rebuked them. But when Jesus saw it, he was indignant and said to them, "Let the children come to me; do not hinder them, for to such belongs the kingdom of God. Truly, I say to you, whoever does not receive the kingdom of God like a child shall not enter it." And he took them in his arms and blessed them, laying his hands on them.

*This is awesome! I think I'm liking this Jesus. Maybe my brother is right. - Emmie*

### The Rich Young Man

And as he was setting out on his journey, a man ran up and knelt before him and asked him, "Good Teacher, what must I do to inherit eternal life?" And Jesus said to him, "Why do you call me good? No one is good except God alone. You know the

*I don't understand why Jesus says this. I thought he was good.*

*- BELLA*

commandments: 'Do not murder, Do not commit adultery, Do not steal, Do not bear false witness, Do not defraud, Honor your father and mother.'" And he said to him, "Teacher, all these I have kept from my youth." And Jesus, looking at him, loved him, and said to him, "You lack one thing: go, sell all that you have and give to the poor, and you will have treasure in heaven; and come, follow me." Disheartened by the saying, he went away sorrowful, for he had great possessions.

*"Jesus loved him." That's awesome! I don't think I noticed that before. — Tayden*

*I don't have any. — Bella*

And Jesus looked around and said to his disciples, "How difficult it will be for those who have wealth to enter the kingdom of God!" And the disciples were amazed at his words. But Jesus said to them again, "Children, how difficult it is to enter the kingdom of God! It is easier for a camel to go through the eye of a needle than for a rich person to enter the kingdom of God." And they were exceedingly astonished, and said to him, "Then who can be saved?" Jesus looked at them and said, "With man it is impossible, but not with God. For all things are possible with God." Peter began to say to him, "See, we have left everything and followed you." Jesus said, "Truly, I say to you, there is no one who has left house or brothers or sisters or mother or father or children or lands, for my sake and for the gospel, who will not receive a hundredfold now in this time, houses and brothers and

*That's what I'm saying. —JB*

*TRUTH! — Tayden*

*I'll take it. Where do I sign? — Bella*

sisters and mothers and children and lands, with persecutions, and in the age to come eternal life. But many who are first will be last, and the last first."

## Jesus Foretells His Death a Third Time

And they were on the road, going up to Jerusalem, and Jesus was walking ahead of them. And they were amazed, and those who followed were afraid. And taking the twelve again, he began to tell them what was to happen to him, saying, "See, we are going up to Jerusalem, and the Son of Man will be delivered over to the chief priests and the scribes, and they will condemn him to death and deliver him over to the Gentiles. And they will mock him and spit on him, and flog him and kill him. And after three days he will rise." *Blows me away to think Jesus knew everything that was going to happen to him and He still went through with it. Respect! — JB*

## The Request of James and John

And James and John, the sons of Zebedee, came up to him and said to him, "Teacher, we want you to do for us whatever we ask of you." And he said to them, "What do you want me to do for you?" And they said to him, "Grant us to sit, one at your right hand and one at your left, in your glory." Jesus said to them, *This seems like a big thing to ask. — Emmie* "You do not know what you are asking. Are you able to drink the cup that I drink, or to be baptized with the baptism with which

I am baptized?" And they said to him, "We are able." And Jesus said to them, "The cup that I drink you will drink, and with the baptism with which I am baptized, you will be baptized, but to sit at my right hand or at my left is not mine to grant, but it is for those for whom it has been prepared." And when the ten heard it, they began to be indignant at James and John. And Jesus called them to him and said to them, "You know that those who are considered rulers of the Gentiles lord it over them, and their great ones exercise authority over them. But it shall not be so among you. But whoever would be great among you must be your servant, and whoever would be first among you must be slave of all. For even the Son of Man came not to be served but to serve, and to give his life as a ransom for many."

*I wonder who that is? — Bella*

*This is what gets me. Jesus came to give his life for people. Why? I'm not sure we're worth it. — JB*

*He thinks you are definitely worth it and so do I. — Mr B*

## Jesus Heals Blind Bartimaeus

And they came to Jericho. And as he was leaving Jericho with his disciples and a great crowd, Bartimaeus, a blind beggar, the son of Timaeus, was sitting by the roadside. And when he heard that it was Jesus of Nazareth, he began to cry out and say, "Jesus, Son of David, have mercy on me!" And many rebuked him, telling him to be silent. But he cried out all the more, "Son of David, have mercy on me!" And Jesus stopped and said, "Call him." And they called the blind man, saying to him, "Take heart. Get up; he is calling you." And throwing off his cloak, he sprang up and came

*They told him shut up? Harsh! — Emmie*

*I wonder if He'd stop for me? — Bella*

to Jesus. And Jesus said to him, "What do you want me to do for you?" And the blind man said to him, "Rabbi, let me recover my sight." And Jesus said to him, "Go your way; your faith has made you well." And immediately he recovered his sight and followed him on the way.

*I want a real life Jesus! —Bella*

# CHAPTER 11
### The Triumphal Entry

Now when they drew near to Jerusalem, to Bethphage and Bethany, at the Mount of Olives, Jesus sent two of his disciples and said to them, "Go into the village in front of you, and immediately as you enter it you will find a colt tied, on which no one has ever sat. Untie it and bring it. If anyone says to you, 'Why are you doing this?' say, 'The Lord has need of it and will send it back here immediately.'" And they went away and found a colt tied at a door outside in the street, and they untied it. And some of those standing there said to them, "What are you doing, untying the colt?" And they told them what Jesus had said, and they let them go. And they brought the colt to Jesus and threw their cloaks on it, and he sat on it. And many spread their cloaks on the road, and others spread leafy branches that they had cut from the fields. And those who went before and those who followed were shouting, "Hosanna! Blessed is he who comes in the name of the Lord! Blessed is the coming kingdom of our

*Jesus only rides Unused Donkeys. Ha Ha. – Tayden*

*Dude! Someone's stealing my donkey! Citizens arrest! – JB*

*Why put their cloaks on the ground? – Emmie*

father David! Hosanna in the highest!"

*I think they finally realized who He was.*
*—Bella*

And he entered Jerusalem and went into the temple. And when he had looked around at everything, as it was already late, he went out to Bethany with the twelve.

### Jesus Curses the Fig Tree

On the following day, when they came from Bethany, he was hungry. And seeing in the distance a fig tree in leaf, he went to see if he could find anything on it. When he came to it, he found nothing but leaves, for it was not the season for figs. And he said to it, "May no one ever eat fruit from you again." And his disciples heard it.

*Why didn't he already know it didn't have fruit on it? He's God, right? Then he curses it?*
*— JB*

### Jesus Cleanses the Temple

And they came to Jerusalem. And he entered the temple and began to drive out those who sold and those who bought in the temple, and he overturned the tables of the money-changers and the seats of those who sold pigeons. And he would not allow anyone to carry anything through the temple. And he was teaching them and saying to them, "Is it not written, 'My house shall be called a house of prayer for all the nations'? But

*Ticked off again.*
*—Emmie*

*Prayer for all nations. Our church is like that.*
*—Tayden*

you have made it a den of robbers." And the chief priests and
the scribes heard it and were seeking a way to destroy him, for
they feared him, because all the crowd was astonished at his
teaching. And when evening came they went out of the city.

*They sure don't like him very much. I know what it's like – Bella*

## The Lesson from the Withered Fig Tree

As they passed by in the morning, they saw the fig tree withered
away to its roots. And Peter remembered and said to him,
"Rabbi, look! The fig tree that you cursed has withered." And
Jesus answered them, "Have faith in God. Truly, I say to you,
whoever says to this mountain, 'Be taken up and thrown into the
sea,' and does not doubt in his heart, but believes that what he
says will come to pass, it will be done for him. Therefore I tell
you, whatever you ask in prayer, believe that you have received
it, and it will be yours. And whenever you stand praying, forgive,
if you have anything against anyone, so that your Father also
who is in heaven may forgive you your trespasses."

*"Hmmm…" – JB*

## The Authority of Jesus Challenged

And they came again to Jerusalem. And as he was walking in the
temple, the chief priests and the scribes and the elders came
to him, and they said to him, "By what authority are you doing
these things, or who gave you this authority to do them?" Jesus

said to them, "I will ask you one question; answer me, and I will tell you by what authority I do these things. Was the baptism of John from heaven or from man? Answer me." And they discussed it with one another, saying, "If we say, 'From heaven,' he will say, 'Why then did you not believe him?' But shall we say, 'From man'?"—they were afraid of the people, for they all held that John really was a prophet. So they answered Jesus, "We do not know." And Jesus said to them, "Neither will I tell you by what authority I do these things."

## CHAPTER 12
### The Parable of the Tenants

And he began to speak to them in parables. "A man planted a vineyard and put a fence around it and dug a pit for the winepress and built a tower, and leased it to tenants and went into another country. When the season came, he sent a servant to the tenants to get from them some of the fruit of the vineyard. And they took him and beat him and sent him away empty-handed. Again he sent to them another servant, and they struck him on the head and treated him shamefully. And he sent another, and him they killed. And so with many others: some they beat, and some they killed. He had still one other, a beloved (son) Finally he sent him to them, saying, 'They will respect my son.' But those tenants said to one another, 'This is the heir. Come, let us kill him, and the inheritance will be ours.' And they took him and killed him and threw him out of the vineyard. What will the owner of the vineyard do? He will come and destroy the tenants and give the vineyard to others. Have you not read this Scripture:

> "'The stone that the builders rejected
>     has become the cornerstone;
> this was the Lord's doing,
>     and it is marvelous in our eyes'?"

And they were seeking to arrest him but feared the people, for they perceived that he had told the parable against them. So they left him and went away.

**Paying Taxes to Caesar**

And they sent to him some of the Pharisees and some of the Herodians, to trap him in his talk. And they came and said to him, "Teacher, we know that you are true and do not care about anyone's opinion. For you are not swayed by appearances, but

*[Handwritten margin notes:]*
*I'm thinking the son is supposed to be Jesus in this story. —Tayden*

*Our pastor said this about Jesus. —Tayden*

*They seem scared of Him. —Emmie*

*Trying to trick Him again. These guys don't learn. —JB*

truly teach the way of God. Is it lawful to pay taxes to Caesar, or not? Should we pay them, or should we not?" But, knowing their hypocrisy, he said to them, "Why put me to the test? Bring me a denarius and let me look at it." And they brought one. And he said to them, "Whose likeness and inscription is this?" They said to him, "Caesar's." Jesus said to them, "Render to Caesar the things that are Caesar's, and to God the things that are God's." And they marveled at him.

*Isn't everything God's? -Bella*

### The Sadducees Ask About the Resurrection

And Sadducees came to him, who say that there is no resurrection. And they asked him a question, saying, "Teacher, Moses wrote for us that if a man's brother dies and leaves a wife, but leaves no child, the man must take the widow and raise up offspring for his brother. There were seven brothers; the first took a wife, and when he died left no offspring. And the second took her, and died, leaving no offspring. And the third likewise. And the seven left no offspring. Last of all the woman also died. In the resurrection, when they rise again, whose wife will she be? For the seven had her as wife."

*That is some weird stuff right there! - JB*

*Seriously? - JB*

Jesus said to them, "Is this not the reason you are wrong, because you know neither the Scriptures nor the power of God? For when they rise from the dead, they neither marry nor are given in marriage, but are like angels in heaven. And as for the dead being raised, have you not read in the book of Moses, in the passage about the bush, how God spoke to him, saying, 'I am the God of Abraham, and the God of Isaac, and the God of Jacob'? He is not God of the dead, but of the living. You are quite wrong."

## The Great Commandment

And one of the scribes came up and heard them disputing with one another, and seeing that he answered them well, asked him, "Which commandment is the most important of all?" Jesus answered, "The most important is, 'Hear, O Israel: The Lord our God, the Lord is one. And you shall love the Lord your God with all your heart and with all your soul and with all your mind and with all your strength.' The second is this: 'You shall love your neighbor as yourself.' There is no other commandment greater than these." And the scribe said to him, "You are right, Teacher. You have truly said that he is one, and there is no other besides him. And to love him with all the heart and with all the understanding and with all the strength, and to love one's neighbor as oneself, is much more than all whole burnt offerings and sacrifices." And when Jesus saw that he answered wisely, he said to him, "You are not far from the kingdom of God." And after that no one dared to ask him any more questions.

*I wish everyone did this. + this. - BELLA*

*Because he schooled them over and over. - Tayden*

## Whose Son Is the Christ?

And as Jesus taught in the temple, he said, "How can the scribes say that the Christ is the son of David? David himself, in the Holy Spirit, declared,

> "'The Lord said to my Lord,
> "Sit at my right hand,
>     until I put your enemies under your feet."'

David himself calls him Lord. So how is he his son?" And the great throng heard him gladly.

*→ I think I'd listen too. - Emmie*

## Beware of the Scribes

*Jesus doesn't like them either. I'm with him. I don't like people who think they're better than everyone. - Bella*

And in his teaching he said, "Beware of the scribes, who like to walk around in long robes and like greetings in the marketplaces and have the best seats in the synagogues and the places of honor at feasts, who devour widows' houses and for a pretense make long prayers. They will receive the greater condemnation."

## The Widow's Offering

And he sat down opposite the treasury and watched the people putting money into the offering box. Many rich people put in large sums. And a poor widow came and put in two small copper coins, which make a penny. And he called his disciples to him and said to them, "Truly, I say to you, this poor widow has put in more than all those who are contributing to the offering box. For they all contributed out of their abundance, but she out of her poverty has put in everything she had, all she had to live on."

*WOW. – Bella*

# CHAPTER 13
## Jesus Foretells Destruction of the Temple
And as he came out of the temple, one of his disciples said to him, "Look, Teacher, what wonderful stones and what wonderful buildings!" And Jesus said to him, "Do you see these great buildings? There will not be left here one stone upon another that will not be thrown down."

## Signs of the End of the Age
And as he sat on the Mount of Olives opposite the temple, Peter and James and John and Andrew asked him privately, "Tell us, when will these things be, and what will be the sign when all these things are about to be accomplished?" And Jesus began to say to them, "See that no one leads you astray. Many will come in my name, saying, 'I am he!' and they will lead many astray. And when you hear of wars and rumors of wars, do not be alarmed. This must take place, but the end is not yet. For nation will rise

*My brother says we're close to the end times. It kind of feels like it, too. – Emmie*

*This sounds like the daily news – Emmie*

against nation, and kingdom against kingdom. There will be earthquakes in various places; there will be famines. These are but the beginning of the birth pains.

"But be on your guard. For they will deliver you over to councils, and you will be beaten in synagogues, and you will stand before governors and kings for my sake, to bear witness before them. And the gospel must first be proclaimed to all nations. And when they bring you to trial and deliver you over, do not be anxious beforehand what you are to say, but say whatever is given you in that hour, for it is not you who speak, but the Holy Spirit. And brother will deliver brother over to death, and the father his child, and children will rise against parents and have them put to death. And you will be hated by all for my name's sake. But the one who endures to the end will be saved. *Sounds like some rough times ahead. — JB*

### The Abomination of Desolation

"But when you see the abomination of desolation standing where he ought not to be (let the reader understand), then let those who are in Judea flee to the mountains. Let the one who is on the housetop not go down, nor enter his house, to take anything out, and let the one who is in the field not turn back to take his cloak. And alas for women who are pregnant and for those who are nursing infants in those days! Pray that it may not happen in winter. For in those days there will be such tribulation as has not been from the beginning of the creation that God created until now, and never will be. And if the Lord had not cut short the days, no human being would be saved. But for the sake of the elect, whom he chose, he shortened the days. And then if anyone says to you, 'Look, here is the Christ!' or 'Look, there he is!' do not believe it. For false christs and false prophets will arise and perform signs and wonders, to lead astray, if possible, the elect. But be on guard; I have told you all things beforehand.

*This scares me. - Emmie*

### The Coming of the Son of Man

"But in those days, after that tribulation, the sun will be darkened, and the moon will not give its light, and the stars will be falling from heaven, and the powers in the heavens will be shaken. And then they will see the Son of Man coming in clouds with great power and glory. And then he will send out the angels and gather his elect from the four winds, from the ends of the earth to the ends of heaven.

*I'm ready. - Tayden*

### The Lesson of the Fig Tree

"From the fig tree learn its lesson: as soon as its branch becomes tender and puts out its leaves, you know that summer is near.

So also, when you see these things taking place, you know that he is near, at the very gates. Truly, I say to you, this generation will not pass away until all these things take place. Heaven and earth will pass away, but my words will not pass away.

*something tells me this might happen in my lifetime. — BELLA*

### No One Knows That Day or Hour

*aren't people picking dates all the time? What do I need to do to be ready? — JB*

"But concerning that day or that hour, no one knows, not even the angels in heaven, nor the Son, but only the Father. Be on guard, keep awake. For you do not know when the time will come. It is like a man going on a journey, when he leaves home and puts his servants in charge, each with his work, and commands the doorkeeper to stay awake. Therefore stay awake—for you do not know when the master of the house will come, in the evening, or at midnight, or when the rooster crows, or in the morning— lest he come suddenly and find you asleep. And what I say to you I say to all: Stay awake."

# CHAPTER 14
### The Plot to Kill Jesus

It was now two days before the Passover and the Feast of Unleavened Bread. And the chief priests and the scribes were seeking how to arrest him by stealth and kill him, for they said, "Not during the feast, lest there be an uproar from the people."

*I really don't like these guys. — BELLA*

## Jesus Anointed at Bethany

And while he was at Bethany in the house of Simon the leper, as he was reclining at table, a woman came with an alabaster flask of ointment of pure nard, very costly, and she broke the flask and poured it over his head. There were some who said to themselves indignantly, "Why was the ointment wasted like that? For this ointment could have been sold for more than three hundred denarii and given to the poor." And they scolded her. But Jesus said, "Leave her alone. Why do you trouble her? She has done a beautiful thing to me. For you always have the poor with you, and whenever you want, you can do good for them. But you will not always have me. She has done what she could; she has anointed my body beforehand for burial. And truly, I say to you, wherever the gospel is proclaimed in the whole world, what she has done will be told in memory of her."

*I'd sell it on ebay. - JB*

*I think it was beautiful. - Bella*

*Cool way to be remembered - Emmie*

## Judas to Betray Jesus

Then Judas Iscariot, who was one of the twelve, went to the chief priests in order to betray him to them. And when they heard it, they were glad and promised to give him money. And he sought an opportunity to betray him.

*Been there. Tough to find friends that won't stab you in the back. Seems like Jesus goes through a bunch of bad stuff. - Bella*

## The Passover with the Disciples

And on the first day of Unleavened Bread, when they sacrificed the Passover lamb, his disciples said to him, "Where will you have us go and prepare for you to eat the Passover?" And he sent two of his disciples and said to them, "Go into the city, and a man carrying a jar of water will meet you. Follow him, and wherever he enters, say to the master of the house, 'The Teacher says, Where is my guest room, where I may eat the Passover with my disciples?' And he will show you a large upper room furnished and ready; there prepare for us." And the disciples set out and went to the city and found it just as he had told them, and they prepared the Passover.

And when it was evening, he came with the twelve. And as they were reclining at table and eating, Jesus said, "Truly, I say to you, one of you will betray me, one who is eating with me." They began to be sorrowful and to say to him one after another, "Is it I?" He said to them, "It is one of the twelve, one who is dipping bread into the dish with me. For the Son of Man goes as it is written of him, but woe to that man by whom the Son of Man is betrayed! It would have been better for that man if he had not been born."

*I'm amazed at stories like this. Jesus had this all set up ahead of time.*
*— Jayden*

*Calling him out.*
*— JB*

*Bet it was tense!*
*— Bella*

## Institution of the Lord's Supper

And as they were eating, he took bread, and after blessing it broke it and gave it to them, and said, "Take; this is my body." And he took a cup, and when he had given thanks he gave it to them, and they all drank of it. And he said to them, "This is my blood of the covenant, which is poured out for many. Truly, I say to you, I will not drink again of the fruit of the vine until that day when I drink it new in the kingdom of God."

*They drank from the same cup? Nasty! — Bella*

## Jesus Foretells Peter's Denial

And when they had sung a hymn, they went out to the Mount of Olives. And Jesus said to them, "You will all fall away, for it is written, 'I will strike the shepherd, and the sheep will be scattered.' But after I am raised up, I will go before you to Galilee." Peter said to him, "Even though they all fall away, I will not." And Jesus said to him, "Truly, I tell you, this very night, before the rooster crows twice, you will deny me three times." But he said emphatically, "If I must die with you, I will not deny you." And they all said the same.

*Three years of being with Jesus and they're all going to leave Him. I never plan to leave Him. — Tayden*

*I don't turn my back on friends. If I ever decide to follow Christ, I'm in it until the end. — JB*

## Jesus Prays in Gethsemane

And they went to a place called Gethsemane. And he said to

his disciples, "Sit here while I pray." And he took with him Peter and James and John, and began to be greatly distressed and troubled. And he said to them, "My soul is very sorrowful, even to death. Remain here and watch." And going a little farther, he fell on the ground and prayed that, if it were possible, the hour might pass from him. And he said, "Abba, Father, all things are possible for you. Remove this cup from me. Yet not what I will, but what you will." And he came and found them sleeping, and he said to Peter, "Simon, are you asleep? Could you not watch one hour? Watch and pray that you may not enter into temptation. The spirit indeed is willing, but the flesh is weak." And again he went away and prayed, saying the same words. And again he came and found them sleeping, for their eyes were very heavy, and they did not know what to answer him. And he came the third time and said to them, "Are you still sleeping and taking your rest? It is enough; the hour has come. The Son of Man is betrayed into the hands of sinners. Rise, let us be going; see, my betrayer is at hand."

*I didn't know Jesus tried to get out of it. – Bella*

*Same guy who said he'd never leave Jesus is sleeping on the job. – Emmie*

*3 Times! Seriously dude! – Tayden*

## Betrayal and Arrest of Jesus

And immediately, while he was still speaking, Judas came, one of the twelve, and with him a crowd with swords and clubs, from the chief priests and the scribes and the elders. Now the betrayer had given them a sign, saying, "The one I will kiss is the man. Seize him and lead him away under guard." And when he came, he went up to him at once and said, "Rabbi!" And he kissed him. And they laid hands on him and seized him. But one of those who stood by drew his sword and struck the servant of the high priest and cut off his ear. And Jesus said to them, "Have you come out as against a robber, with swords and clubs to capture me? Day after day I was with you in the temple teaching, and you did not seize me. But let the Scriptures be fulfilled." And they all left him and fled.

*I've had a few guys betray me, but not by kissing me but kissing someone else. - Emmie*

*Dude, I'm cutting someone too, but probably Judas, not the slave guy. —JB*

*I know the feeling. – BeLLA*

## A Young Man Flees

And a young man followed him, with nothing but a linen cloth about his body. And they seized him, but he left the linen cloth and ran away naked. *Why is this even in here? -Tayden*

## Jesus Before the Council

*Wonder how many of us follow Jesus at a distance. – Mr B*

And they led Jesus to the high priest. And all the chief priests and the elders and the scribes came together. And Peter had followed him at a distance, right into the courtyard of the high priest. And he was sitting with the guards and warming himself at the fire. Now the chief priests and the whole council were seeking testimony against Jesus to put him to death, but they found none. For many bore false witness against him, but their testimony did not agree. And some stood up and bore false witness against him, saying, "We heard him say, 'I will destroy this temple that is made with hands, and in three days I will build another, not made with hands.'" Yet even about this their testimony did not agree. And the high priest stood up in the midst and asked Jesus, "Have you no answer to make? What is it that these men testify against you?" But he remained silent and made no answer. Again the high priest asked him, "Are you the Christ, the Son of the Blessed?" And Jesus said, "I am, and you will see the Son of Man seated at the right hand of Power, and coming with the clouds of heaven." And the high priest tore his garments and said, "What further witnesses do we need? You have heard his blasphemy. What is your decision?" And they all condemned him as deserving death. And some began to spit on him and to cover his face and to strike him, saying to him, "Prophesy!" And the guards received him with blows.

*It's kind of funny that no one can get their stories straight — Emmie*

*Takes the 5th —JB*

*Jesus actually says He is the Messiah. This seems like a big moment. — Tayden*

*Why beat him? — Bella*

### Peter Denies Jesus

And as Peter was below in the courtyard, one of the servant girls of the high priest came, and seeing Peter warming himself, she looked at him and said, "You also were with the Nazarene, Jesus." But he denied it, saying, "I neither know nor understand

*Once.*

what you mean." And he went out into the gateway and the
rooster crowed. And the servant girl saw him and began again
to say to the bystanders, "This man is one of them." But again
he denied it. And after a little while the bystanders again said

*Twice.*

to Peter, "Certainly you are one of them, for you are a Galilean."
But he began to invoke a curse on himself and to swear, "I do not
know this man of whom you speak." And immediately the rooster
crowed a second time. And Peter remembered how Jesus had said

to him, "Before the rooster crows twice, you will deny me three
times." And he broke down and wept. *

*Three times!*
*Jesus nailed it.*
*—JB*

*God is drawn to broken hearts.*
*— Mr. B*

## CHAPTER 15
### Jesus Delivered to Pilate

And as soon as it was morning, the chief priests held a
consultation with the elders and scribes and the whole council.
And they bound Jesus and led him away and delivered him over
to Pilate. And Pilate asked him, "Are you the King of the Jews?"
And he answered him, "You have said so." And the chief priests
accused him of many things. And Pilate again asked him, "Have
you no answer to make? See how many charges they bring against
you." But Jesus made no further answer, so that Pilate was
amazed.

*Why doesn't He defend Himself? Speak up!*
*— Emmie*

## Pilate Delivers Jesus to Be Crucified

Now at the feast he used to release for them one prisoner for whom they asked. And among the rebels in prison, who had committed murder in the insurrection, there was a man called Barabbas. And the crowd came up and began to ask Pilate to do as he usually did for them. And he answered them, saying, "Do you want me to release for you the King of the Jews?" For he perceived that it was out of envy that the chief priests had delivered him up. But the chief priests stirred up the crowd to have him release for them Barabbas instead. And Pilate again said to them, "Then what shall I do with the man you call the King of the Jews?" And they cried out again, "Crucify him." And Pilate said to them, "Why? What evil has he done?" But they shouted all the more, "Crucify him." So Pilate, wishing to satisfy the crowd, released for them Barabbas, and having scourged Jesus, he delivered him to be crucified.

*They wanted to let a criminal go instead of Jesus. That's wrong. —Bella*

*For What? Helping people? - Emmie*

*They beat Him before they killed Him? This is starting to tick me off. — JB*

## Jesus Is Mocked

And the soldiers led him away inside the palace (that is, the governor's headquarters), and they called together the whole battalion. And they clothed him in a purple cloak, and twisting together a crown of thorns, they put it on him. And they began to salute him, "Hail, King of the Jews!" And they were striking his head with a reed and spitting on him and kneeling down in

*Leave him alone! - Emmie*

homage to him. And when they had mocked him, they stripped him of the purple cloak and put his own clothes on him. And they led him out to crucify him.

## The Crucifixion

And they compelled a passerby, Simon of Cyrene, who was coming in from the country, the father of Alexander and Rufus, to carry his cross. And they brought him to the place called Golgotha (which means Place of a Skull). And they offered him wine mixed with myrrh, but he did not take it. And they crucified him and divided his garments among them, <u>casting lots for them</u>, to decide what each should take. And it was the third hour when they crucified him. And the inscription of the charge against him read, "The King of the Jews." And with him they crucified two robbers, one on his right and one on his left. And those who passed by derided him, wagging their heads and saying, "Aha! You who would destroy the temple and rebuild it in three days, save yourself, and come down from the cross!" So also the chief priests with the scribes mocked him to one another, saying, "He saved others; he <u>cannot save himself</u>. Let the Christ, the King of Israel, come down now from the cross that we may see and believe." Those who were crucified with him also reviled him.

*I would've volunteered. — Bella*

*I think this was a prophecy in the Old Testament. — Tayden*

*I've read this whole thing and He didn't do anything wrong. This is sick! Why doesn't He just crush them? — JB*

*The prophecies had to be fulfilled and He had to die for our sins. It was the only way to give you and I hope and salvation. — Mr. B*

## The Death of Jesus

And when the sixth hour had come, there was darkness over the whole land until the ninth hour. And at the ninth hour Jesus cried with a loud voice, "Eloi, Eloi, lema sabachthani?" which means, "My God, my God, why have you forsaken me?" And some of the bystanders hearing it said, "Behold, he is calling Elijah." And someone ran and filled a sponge with sour wine, put it on a reed and gave it to him to drink, saying, "Wait, let us see whether Elijah will come to take him down." And Jesus uttered a loud cry and breathed his last. And the curtain of the temple was torn in two, from top to bottom. And when the centurion, who stood facing him, saw that in this way he breathed his last, he said, "Truly this man was the Son of God!"

There were also women looking on from a distance, among whom were Mary Magdalene, and Mary the mother of James the younger and of Joses, and Salome. When he was in Galilee, they followed him and ministered to him, and there were also many other women who came up with him to Jerusalem.

## Jesus Is Buried

And when evening had come, since it was the day of Preparation, that is, the day before the Sabbath, Joseph of Arimathea, a respected member of the council, who was also himself looking for the kingdom of God, took courage and went to Pilate and asked for the body of Jesus. Pilate was surprised to hear that he should have already died. And summoning the centurion, he asked him whether he was already dead. And when he learned from the centurion that he was dead, he granted the corpse to Joseph. And Joseph bought a linen shroud, and taking him down, wrapped him in the linen shroud and laid him in a tomb that had been cut out of the rock. And he rolled a stone against the entrance of the tomb. Mary Magdalene and Mary the mother of Joses saw where he was laid.

*This reminds me of the woman who poured perfume on Jesus feet. This is a beautiful thing for Joseph to do. —Bella*

## CHAPTER 16
### The Resurrection
When the Sabbath was past, Mary Magdalene, Mary the mother of James, and Salome bought spices, so that they might go and anoint him. And very early on the first day of the week, when the sun had risen, they went to the tomb. And they were saying to one another, "Who will roll away the stone for us from the entrance of the tomb?" And looking up, they saw that the stone had been rolled back—it was very large. And entering the tomb, they saw a young man sitting on the right side, dressed in a white robe, and they were alarmed. And he said to them, "Do not be alarmed. You seek Jesus of Nazareth, who was crucified. He has

*Why would they put spices on a dead body? —Emmie*

*So they were hoping someone would be there to move the stone? Done already. —Bella* risen; he is not here. See the place where they laid him. But go, tell his disciples and Peter that he is going before you to Galilee. There you will see him, just as he told you." And they went out and fled from the tomb, for trembling and astonishment had seized them, and they said nothing to anyone, for they were afraid.

*I don't know what to say except God forgive me. I've never really seen all of this before. Jesus please forgive me somehow. I'm messed up. Please.*
*JB*

*Me too JB. I want to follow Him.*
*- Emmie*

## Jesus Appears to Mary Magdalene

Now when he rose early on the first day of the week, he appeared first to Mary Magdalene, from whom he had cast out seven demons. She went and told those who had been with him, as they mourned and wept. But when they heard that he was alive and had been seen by her, they would not believe it.

*I think it would be hard to believe it was him when you saw him die.*
*- Tayden*

## Jesus Appears to Two Disciples

After these things he appeared in another form to two of them, as they were walking into the country. And they went back and told the rest, but they did not believe them.

## The Great Commission

Afterward he appeared to the eleven themselves as they were reclining at table, and he rebuked them for their unbelief and hardness of heart, because they had not believed those who saw him after he had risen. And he said to them, "Go into all the world and proclaim the gospel to the whole creation. <u>Whoever believe</u>s and is baptized will be saved, but whoever does not believe will be condemned. And these signs will accompany those who believe: in my name they will cast out demons; they will speak in new tongues; they will pick up serpents with their hands; and if they drink any deadly poison, it will not hurt them; they will lay their hands on the sick, and they will recover."

*I guess I believe now.*
*— JB*

So then the Lord Jesus, after he had spoken to them, was taken up into heaven and sat down at the right hand of God. And they went out and preached everywhere, while the Lord worked with them and confirmed the message by accompanying signs.

*Texted my brother. He's crazy excited and wants to help me become a Christian.*
*- Emmie*

*I want to believe Jesus really does love me. Things are just so messed up. God, can you please send someone to help me?*
*-Bella*

HAS GOD OPENED YOUR EYES TO THE TRUTH? IS HE DOING SOMETHING IN YOUR HEART?

NOW IS YOUR CHANCE TO MAKE A CRUCIAL DECISION ABOUT YOUR LIFE AND YOUR FUTURE.

Jesus asked an important question when He was here on Earth:

"Who do YOU say that I am?"

# WHO DO YOU SAY JESUS IS?

Is He the son of God?  Did He live without sin?  Did He pay the penalty for Your sin, breaking the curse?  Did He rise again from the dead?

He was either crazy, allowing Himself to be killed when He could have easily avoided it, or He was and is the son of God.

### Who do You say Jesus is?
a. Son of God who lived a sinless life and died to pay for my sin
b. Crazy peasant preacher who died for nothing
c. _____

The next most important question is:

## WHO ARE YOU?

Are you a sinner who has inherited the curse placed on all people? Is your sin keeping you from God? What is your eternal destination, heaven or hell?

The Bible says in John 3:18 that if you don't believe in who Jesus is and what He has done for you, then right now you stand condemned to an eternity in hell.

**Who are you?**
   a. Under the curse, condemned to hell without Jesus
   b. Doing fine without God and not worried about when I die
   c. _____

## SO, WHAT WILL YOU DO?

Jesus Said ,"Come Follow Me."

If you agree with God, (confess) that you are a sinner who desperately needs your sins paid for with the ultimate sacrifice, there is good news.

In the Bible, in the book of 1 John, God says: "If you confess your sins, He is faithful and just to forgive you."

God can forgive you based on the sacrifice of Jesus.

In the Bible, in the book of Romans God says:

"If you confess with your mouth Jesus is Lord and believe in your heart that God raised Him from the dead, you will be saved."

It doesn't matter who you are or what you've done. You don't have to clean up your life first. If God has opened your eyes to see your sin and His love for you, He is waiting with open arms for you. Run to Him now. Wherever you are and whatever you're doing, surrender your life to Him now.

*Can't stop crying. God somehow helped me see what my brother sees.*
*– Emmie*

## How To Become a Child of God (and get to Heaven)

1. Confess to God you are a sinner.
   SAY "God, I admit I'm a sinner"

*Can't resist Him anymore. God really did something in me. totally changed my heart. – JB*

2. Tell Him you believe Jesus died to pay the penalty for your sin and rose from the dead to give you new life.
   SAY "I believe Jesus' death on the cross paid the penalty for

my sin and his rising from the dead gives me new life"

3. Tell Him that you trust Jesus to forgive you and give you a fresh start.
   SAY "God, I trust you to forgive my sins and give me a fresh start"

4. Ask Him to come and live in you through His spirit.
   SAY "God, please come and live in me by your Holy Spirit"

5. Commit your life to following Him and His ways.
   SAY "I commit my life to follow Your ways, not my ways. Please help me do that. Amen."

*Not always easy to follow, but God's ways are always best. — Tayden*

If you are now a follower of Jesus Christ, He has given you a new heart and the Bible says your name is now written in the Lamb's Book of Life.

Sign your name below with today's date to remember the day God gave you a new heart and a new life.

Child of God/Follower of Jesus (Your Name)

_____

Today's Date

_____

# FIRST STEPS

•Contact the person who gave you The Life Book and let them know God has saved you. They'll be very happy for you!

•Ask the person who gave you the Life Book to help you get a complete Bible to read.

•Go to church with the person who gave you the Life Book. This will help you in your new life of following Jesus.

•Read a little bit of your Bible every day.

•Talk to God every day.  Let him know your concerns, your worries, and ask for His help and direction in your new life.

•Find friends who follow Jesus.

•Tell others how God changed your heart, rescued you from your sin, gave you a new life and a new purpose as a follower of Jesus.

# HELP!

THIS SECTION IS FOR EVERYONE WHO HAS EVER WISHED
THEY COULD SIT DOWN WITH GOD AND ASK HIM ABOUT
PROBLEMS IN THEIR LIFE. YOU MAY NOT BE STRUGGLING
RIGHT NOW, BUT MAYBE A FRIEND NEEDS YOUR HELP.
HOPEFULLY THESE BIBLE PASSAGES WILL HELP YOU AND
GIVE YOU SOME GUIDANCE.

# RELATIONSHIPS AND SEX

### Am I really in love?

Love is patient and kind; love does not envy or boast; it is not
arrogant or rude. It does not insist on its own way; it is not
irritable or resentful; it does not rejoice at wrongdoing, but
rejoices with the truth. Love bears all things, believes all things,
hopes all things, endures all things.
(1 Corinthians 13:4-7)

> *I haven't really met many guys who
> look at love this way. Most guys
> are totally selfish and prideful. So
> is that even love? Maybe not!*
> *—Bella*

### God Reserves Sex for Marriage?

"Therefore a man shall leave his father and mother and hold
fast to his wife, and the two shall become one flesh." (Ephesians
5:31)

> *Saving myself for
> marriage.*
> *— Emmie*

For this is the will of God, your sanctification: that you abstain
from sexual immorality; that each one of you know how to
control his own body in holiness and honor, not in the passion of
lust like the Gentiles who do not know God;
(1 Thessalonians 4:3-5)

Or do you not know that the unrighteous will not inherit the
kingdom of God? Do not be deceived: neither the sexually
immoral, nor idolaters, nor adulterers, nor men who practice

> *Wow! Didn't
> know the Bible
> said this.*
> *— JB*

homosexuality, nor thieves, nor the greedy, nor drunkards, nor
revilers, nor swindlers will inherit the kingdom of God.
(1 Corinthians 6:9-10)

**How far is too far?**
Flee from sexual immorality. Every other sin a person commits is
outside the body, but the sexually immoral person sins against
his own body. (1 Corinthians 6:18)

# MADE BY GOD AND FOR GOD

I praise you, for I am fearfully and wonderfully made. Wonderful
are your works; my soul knows it very well. My frame was not
hidden from you, when I was being made in secret, intricately
woven in the depths of the earth. Your eyes saw my unformed
substance; in your book were written, every one of them, the
days that were formed for me, when as yet there was none of
them. (Psalm 139:14-16)

*Wish I could see myself like that.*
*—Bella*

*Bella, it's true. God made you beautiful.*
*— Tayden*

But now, O Lord, you are our Father; we are the clay, and you are
our potter; we are all the work of your hand. (Isaiah 64:8)

He is the image of the invisible God, the firstborn of all

creation. For by him all things were created, in heaven and on earth, visible and invisible, whether thrones or dominions or rulers or authorities—all things were created through him and for him. (Colossians 1:15-16)

*That's cool.*
*– j8*

But even the hairs of your head are all numbered. Fear not, therefore; you are of more value than many sparrows. So everyone who acknowledges me before men, I also will acknowledge before my Father who is in heaven, but whoever denies me before men, I also will deny before my Father who is in heaven. (Matthew 10:30-33)

Know that the Lord, he is God! It is he who made us, and we are his; we are his people, and the sheep of his pasture. (Psalm 100:3)

## DEPRESSION / WORRY

Why are you cast down, O my soul, and why are you in turmoil within me? Hope in God; for I shall again praise him, my salvation (Psalm 42:5)

Trust in the Lord with all your heart, and do not lean on your own understanding. In all your ways acknowledge him, and he will make straight your paths. (Proverbs 3:5-6)

May the God of hope fill you with all joy and peace in believing, so that by the power of the Holy Spirit you may abound in hope. (Romans 15:13)

*This one is going to help me BIG TIME - Emmie*

Rejoice in the Lord always; again I will say, Rejoice. Let your reasonableness be known to everyone. The Lord is at hand; do not be anxious about anything, but in everything by prayer and supplication with thanksgiving let your requests be made known to God. And the peace of God, which surpasses all understanding, will guard your hearts and your minds in Christ Jesus. (Philippians 4:4-7)

We are afflicted in every way, but not crushed; perplexed, but not driven to despair; persecuted, but not forsaken; struck down, but not destroyed... So we do not lose heart. Though our outer self is wasting away, our inner self is being renewed day by day. (2 Corinthians 4:8-9, 16)

But they who wait for the Lord shall renew their strength; they shall mount up with wings like eagles; they shall run and not be weary; they shall walk and not faint. (Isaiah 40:31)

# LIVING AS A FOLLOWER OF CHRIST

Therefore, if anyone is in Christ, he is a new creation. The old has passed away; behold, the new has come. (2 Corinthians 5:17)

*NEW!*
*- Emmie*

For to me to live is Christ, and to die is gain. (Philippians 1:21)

I have been crucified with Christ. It is no longer I who live, but Christ who lives in me. And the life I now live in the flesh I live by faith in the Son of God, who loved me and gave himself for me. (Galatians 2:20)

*Goodbye old life.*
*JB*

But whatever gain I had, I counted as loss for the sake of Christ. Indeed, I count everything as loss because of the surpassing worth of knowing Christ Jesus my Lord. For his sake I have suffered the loss of all things and count them as rubbish, in order that I may gain Christ. (Philippians 3:7-8)

*Favorite verse.*
*- Tayden*

"If anyone would come after me, let him deny himself and take up his cross and follow me. For whoever would save his life will lose it, but whoever loses his life for my sake and the gospel's will save it. For what does it profit a man to gain the whole world and forfeit his soul? (Mark 8:34-36)

*It's all worth it.*
*Mr B*

# CHOOSE FRIENDS WISELY

Blessed is the man who walks not in the counsel of the wicked, nor stands in the way of sinners, nor sits in the seat of scoffers; but his delight is in the law of the Lord, and on his law he meditates day and night. (Psalm 1:1-2)

So flee youthful passions and pursue righteousness, faith, love, and peace, along with those who call on the Lord from a pure heart. (2 Timothy 2:22)

Do not be deceived: "Bad company ruins good morals." (1 Corinthians 15:33)   *I could definitely use some new friends.  —Bella*

# HEART AND MIND

You shall love the Lord your God with all your heart and with all your soul and with all your mind. (Matthew 22:37)

Do not love the world or the things in the world. If anyone loves the world, the love of the Father is not in him. For all that is in the world—the desires of the flesh and the desires of the eyes and pride of life—is not from the Father but is from the world. And the world is passing away along with its desires, but whoever does the will of God abides forever. (1 John 2:15-17)

Set your minds on things that are above, not on things that are on earth. (Colossians 3:2)

Do not lay up for yourselves treasures on earth, where moth and rust destroy and where thieves break in and steal, but lay up for yourselves treasures in heaven, where neither moth nor rust destroys and where thieves do not break in and steal. For where your treasure is, there your heart will be also. (Matthew 6:19-21)

Finally, brothers, whatever is true, whatever is honorable, whatever is just, whatever is pure, whatever is lovely, whatever is commendable, if there is any excellence, if there is anything worthy of praise, think about these things. (Philippians 4:8)

God's working on my heart with this one.
 — Tayden

# WHO WILL YOU GIVE THE LIFE BOOK TO?

## PLEASE SHARE THE LIFE BOOK

Jesus said to them, "Go into all the world and proclaim the gospel to the whole creation." (Mark 16:15)

## SHARE YOUR LIFE BOOK STORY

thelifebook.com/share

## WANT TO BRING THE LIFE BOOK TO YOUR AREA?

Ask your youth leader to go to thelifebook.com/youthleaders

## WANT A DIGITAL COPY OF THE LIFE BOOK?

FREE and downloadable...Go to thelifebook.com/read

## LIKE US ON FACEBOOK

facebook.com/thelifebookofficial